To

From

Daddy, Will You Dance with Me?
Copyright © 2006 by Sandra Schoger Foster

Published by J. Countryman®, a division of Thomas Nelson, Inc., Nashville, Tennessee

J. Countryman® is a trademark of Thomas Nelson, Inc.

Designed by Koechel Peterson and Associates, Inc., Minneapolis, Minnesota

Project Editor: Lisa Stilwell

ISBN 1-4041-0350-3

Printed and bound in the United States of America

www.thomasnelson.com | www.jcountryman.com

www.sandraschogerfoster.com

Daddy, Will You Dance with Me?

Celebrating
Special Moments
between Fathers
and Daughters

BY SANDRA SCHOGER FOSTER

Let them praise

his name with dancing...

"Daddy, will you dance with me?" asked Cydney.

He scooped her up in his arms and they twirled and whirled around the room as he hummed into her cheek.

will you dance with me?

She giggled and placed her hands on his face. "I love you, Daddy."

"I love you too, my sweet Cydney girl. And God loves you as though you were the o-o-only one in a-a-all the world to love—and that makes you very special."

Cydney was a flower girl in her aunt's wedding. After the ceremony, she watched the bride and groom dance at their reception. She reached for her father's hand.

Will you dance with me?

Stand on my shoes

"Daddy, will you dance with me?" she asked.

Taking her hand, he said with a smile and a little bow, "Stand on my shoes and hold my hands."

Dance with me . . .

They danced together as if the band were playing for them alone.

"Daddy, when I'm all grown up, will you still dance with me?"

"Of course I will, my sweet Cydney girl. I love you. And God loves you as though you were the o-o-only one in a-a-all the world to love—and that makes you very special."

"Hooray, I'm finally ten!" Cydney shouted as she bounced down the stairs two at a time.

"Daddy, will you dance with me before my friends get here for my party?"

Reaching for her hand, he said with a smile and a little bow, "Do you think you can still dance on my shoes? You're almost grown up now!"

"I want to try, Daddy."

Hold my hands.

"Hold my hands and we'll give it a whirl."

When they started to dance they almost fell down. He caught her, and both of them burst out laughing and had to hold onto each other for support.

I love you,
Birthday Girl

"Follow my lead," he said, and soon they were dancing in step. He hummed into her cheek and whispered, "I love you, Birthday Girl. And God loves you as though you were the only one in all the world to love—and that makes you very special."

"Today Jordyn and I were walking home from school, and when a group of older kids passed us, one of them stuck bubblegum in my hair and then ran away laughing. I thought I was going to like being in junior high," Cydney said to her father with tears in her eyes.

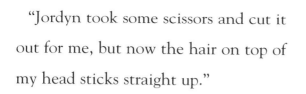

"Jordyn took some scissors and cut it out for me, but now the hair on top of my head sticks straight up."

He cupped her face in his hands. "I'm so sorry they did that to you, honey. You still look wonderful to me!"

You still look wonderful

She sighed. "You always know how to make me feel better. Daddy, will you dance with me?"

They twirled and whirled around the room as he hummed into her cheek.

"I love you, my sweet Cydney girl. And God loves you as though you were the only one in all the world to love—and that makes you very special."

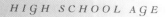

One day when Cydney
came home from high school
she was choking back tears.

"What happened, sweet-
heart?" her father asked.

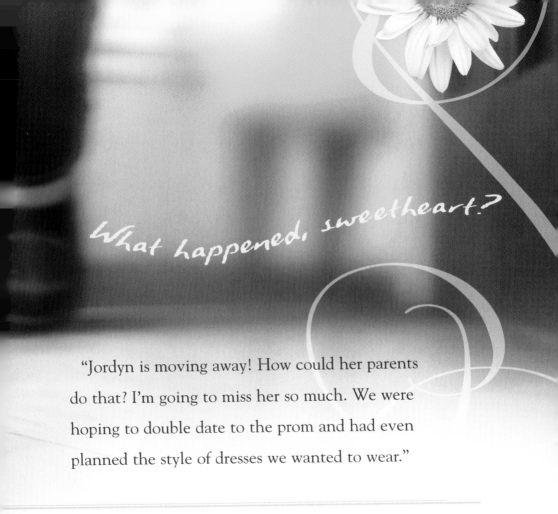

What happened, sweetheart?

"Jordyn is moving away! How could her parents do that? I'm going to miss her so much. We were hoping to double date to the prom and had even planned the style of dresses we wanted to wear."

She sniffled as she plopped down on the couch beside her father. "And what about our plans to room together in college?"

He put his arm around her. "Oh, my sweet Cydney girl. This is really sad news. I can see how much this hurts you."

Oh, my sweet Cydney

Then doing what she always did when she felt
very happy or very sad, Cydney said tearfully,

"Oh, Daddy, will you dance with me?"

...they twirled

and whirled

They twirled and whirled around the room

as he hummed into her cheek.

"It's hard when people we love move away," her father said. "But always remember that I love you, my sweet Cydney girl. And God loves you too, just as though you were the only one in all the world to love—and that makes you very special."

She dried her tears on his sleeve.

"I'm so glad you're here to walk me down the aisle on my wedding day, Daddy."

my wedding day

"It's my greatest joy, my sweet Cydney girl—
and you are a beautiful bride! But just where did
my little girl go?"

I'll always be your little girl

"Even though I don't dance on your shoes anymore, I'll always be your little girl."

At the wedding reception, Cydney danced first with her new husband. Then she turned to her father. "Daddy…"

How did you know...

"Will you dance with me?" he said with a smile as he gave a little bow and took her hand.

"Now how did you know what I was going to ask?" Cydney said with a little laugh.

They twirled and whirled
around the room to the music
of the band.

I'll always love you

"I'll always love you, my sweet Cydney girl. And God will too, just as though you were the only one in all the world to love—and that makes you very special."

Cydney's uncle wanted her and her husband to come work for him in a distant city. After much thought and prayer, they decided the move was right for them. When the moving van had left with all their belongings and the time came for them to say good-bye, Cydney reached for her father's hand.

Daddy, will you . . .

"Daddy, will you dance with me before we leave?"

They twirled and whirled around the empty apartment that echoed with memories of her newlywed years with her husband.

Her voice quivered. "I'll miss dancing with you, Daddy."

"I don't know what I'll do without my sweet Cydney girl. You'll be living so far away. Always remember how much I love you. And God loves you as though you were the only one in all the world to love—and that makes you very special."

. . .remember how much

I love you

Looking into her father's eyes she saw tears splash down onto his cheeks. She had never seen him cry before.

"Daddy," Cydney said when her father came to visit, "meet Jordyn Rose, your new granddaughter!"

"You named her after your childhood friend," he said, taking the tiny baby in his arms and covering her little head with kisses.

Dance with us...

"Daddy, will you dance with us?"

He wrapped his arms around both of them and they gently twirled and whirled around the room. He hummed into baby Jordyn's cheek and whispered, "Child of my heart, do you know that God loves you as though you were the o-o-only one in a-a-all the world to love? And that makes you very special."

"Daddy, your love has been such a gift to me through the years. Thank you for all the dances we've shared, and for always loving me no matter what. I'm so glad that Jordyn can know your special love."

Thank you

for always loving me

She hugged him and saw his eyes well up.

Many years later Cydney made a special trip home to surprise her father on his birthday. She tiptoed into his room where he had nodded off to sleep. Reaching for his familiar hand, she kissed him on the cheek.

"Happy birthday, Daddy!"

His face lit up. "Oh, my sweet Cydney girl!"

"Daddy, will you dance with me?" she said, helping him to stand up.

"How I wish these tired legs could dance again!" he said, leaning on his cane to steady himself.

She wrapped her arm around his shoulder, tossed his cane aside, and took his hand. They twirled and whirled around the room ever so carefully as she hummed into his cheek.

someday we'll dance

together forever

"I still love dancing with you, Daddy. And someday
we'll dance together forever on streets of gold. Until
then, always remember how much I love you. And God
loves you as though you were the o-o-only one in a-a-all
the world to love—and that makes you very special."

59

One rainy afternoon Jordyn and her father were snuggled up on the couch looking at the family photo album. The pages had been turned so many times that the edges curled. Jordyn stopped turning the pages, though, when she got to the pictures of her mommy dancing on her grandfather's shoes.

"Daddy, will you dance with *me?*" Jordyn asked, looking up at him.

snuggled up on the couch

my sweet Jordyn girl